MW01493734

LOCATION AND GEOGRAPHY POSTTEST

Multiple Choice: Write the letter of the correct answer in each blank. (TEN POINTS EACH)

SS.7.G.1.1 Locate the fifty states and their capital cities in addition to the nation's capital on a map.

_____ 1. Where is Washington, D.C. located?
   A. Between New York and Canada
   B. Between Maryland and Virginia
   C. Between California and Arizona
   D. Between Pennsylvania and New Jersey

_____ 2. What is the capital of Georgia?
   A. Atlanta
   B. Columbus
   C. Macon
   D. Savannah

_____ 3. Sacramento is the capital of what state?
   A. Alabama
   B. Alaska
   C. California
   D. Colorado

SS.7.G.2.1 Locate major cultural landmarks that are emblematic of the United States.

_____ 4. The Statue of Liberty is located in what state?
   A. New Hampshire
   B. New Jersey
   C. New Mexico
   D. New York

_____ 5. What cultural landmark is located in Philadelphia?
   A. Liberty Bell
   B. Mount Rushmore
   C. National Aquarium
   D. Washington Monument

_____ 6. In what city is the Alamo?
   A. San Francisco, California
   B. San Diego, California
   C. San Antonio, Texas
   D. San Angelo, Texas

SS.7.G.2.2 Locate major physical landmarks that are emblematic of the United States.

_____ 7. In what state is the Everglades National Park located?
   A. Delaware
   B. Florida
   C. Hawaii
   D. Kansas

_____ 8. What is the tallest mountain in the United States?
   A. Mount McKinley
   B. Mount Whitney
   C. Mount Rainier
   D. Mount Bear

SS.7.G.2.3 Explain how major characteristics, natural resources, climate, and absolute and relative location have influenced settlement, economies, and inter-governmental relations in North America.

_____ 9. The warm climate, rich soil and plentiful rain helped to make farming a major industry in what region that is home to the 'Sun Belt'?
   A. Midwest
   B. Northeast
   C. Pacific
   D. South

SS.7.G.2.4 Describe current major cultural regions of North America.

_____ 10. What states are in the Interior West region?
   A. Arkansas, Tennessee, and South Carolina
   B. Massachusetts, Connecticut, and Maine
   C. Wyoming, New Mexico, and Colorado
   D. Washington, Hawaii, and Oregon

LOCATION AND GEOGRAPHY POSTTEST

Multiple Choice: Write the letter of the correct answer in each blank. (TEN POINTS EACH)

SS.7.G.1.1 Locate the fifty states and their capital cities in addition to the nation's capital on a map.

B   1. Where is Washington, D.C. located?
- A. Between New York and Canada
- **B. Between Maryland and Virginia**
- C. Between California and Arizona
- D. Between Pennsylvania and New Jersey

A   2. What is the capital of Georgia?
- **A. Atlanta**
- B. Columbus
- C. Macon
- D. Savannah

C   3. Sacramento is the capital of what state?
- A. Alabama
- B. Alaska
- **C. California**
- D. Colorado

SS.7.G.2.1 Locate major cultural landmarks that are emblematic of the United States.

D   4. The Statue of Liberty is located in what state?
- A. New Hampshire
- B. New Jersey
- C. New Mexico
- **D. New York**

A   5. What cultural landmark is located in Philadelphia?
- **A. Liberty Bell**
- B. Mount Rushmore
- C. National Aquarium
- D. Washington Monument

C   6. In what city is the Alamo?
- A. San Francisco, California
- B. San Diego, California
- **C. San Antonio, Texas**
- D. San Angelo, Texas

SS.7.G.2.2 Locate major physical landmarks that are emblematic of the United States.

B   7. In what state is the Everglades National Park located?
- A. Delaware
- **B. Florida**
- C. Hawaii
- D. Kansas

A   8. What is the tallest mountain in the United States?
- **A. Mount McKinley**
- B. Mount Whitney
- C. Mount Rainier
- D. Mount Bear

SS.7.G.2.3 Explain how major characteristics, natural resources, climate, and absolute and relative location have influenced settlement, economies, and inter-governmental relations in North America.

D   9. The warm climate, rich soil and plentiful rain helped to make farming a major industry in what region that is home to the 'Sun Belt'?
- A. Midwest
- B. Northeast
- C. Pacific
- **D. South**

SS.7.G.2.4 Describe current major cultural regions of North America.

C   10. What states are in the Interior West region?
- A. Arkansas, Tennessee, and South Carolina
- B. Massachusetts, Connecticut, and Maine
- **C. Wyoming, New Mexico, and Colorado**
- D. Washington, Hawaii, and Oregon

NAME _____

DATE _____

MOD _____

WHAT IS CIVICS POSTTEST

Multiple Choice: Write the letter of the correct answer in each blank. (TEN POINTS EACH)

SS.7.C.2.1 Define the term 'citizen' and identify legal means of becoming a U.S. citizen.

_____ 1. What is the legal process for becoming a U.S. citizen?
   A. Confederation
   B. Initiation
   C. Mediation
   D. Naturalization

_____ 2. What amendment to the U.S. constitution grants citizenship to any person who is born in the United States, the District of Columbia, or American territories?
   A. 13th Amendment
   B. 14th Amendment
   C. 15th Amendment
   D. 16th Amendment

_____ 3. Which of the following is a qualification for an immigrant to become a U.S. citizen?
   A. Must be 21 years of age or older
   B. Must be able to read and write in two languages
   C. Must have been a permanent, legal resident for five years
   D. Must have been a registered voter for at least seven years

_____ 4. Unlike citizens, resident aliens are not able to _____ in the United States.
   A. Pay taxes
   B. Own property
   C. Vote in elections
   D. Attend public schools

_____ 5. In 1920, which group of Americans gained the right to vote with the Nineteenth Amendment?
   A. Women
   B. Hispanics
   C. Residents of Washington, D.C.
   D. Men who did not own property

SS.7.C.2.2 Evaluate the obligations citizens have to obey laws, pay taxes, defend the nation, and serve on juries.

_____ 6. Which of the following is an example of a U.S. citizen's responsibility?
   A. Vote in elections
   B. Attend school
   C. Obey the law
   D. Pay taxes

_____ 7. What is the purpose of the Selective Service System (SSS)?
   A. Identifies men who may be eligible to be drafted into military service if needed
   B. Identifies men who may be eligible to serve on a jury for a criminal trial
   C. Identifies men and women who may be needed for public service
   D. Identifies men and women who wish to work in education

_____ 8. What is the voting age in the United States?
   A. 16
   B. 18
   C. 21
   D. 25

_____ 9. What is the difference between duties and responsibility?
   A. Duties are actions, like paying taxes, that are required by law.
   B. Duties are actions, like volunteering, that are not required by law.
   C. Duties are actions, like voting, that are required of all U.S. citizens.
   D. Duties are actions, like volunteering, that are not required of all U.S. citizens.

EXTENDED RESPONSE: Use the primary source below to answer the question. (10 POINTS)

"The ultimate rulers of our democracy are not a President and Senators and Congressmen and government officials but the voters of this country." – Franklin D. Roosevelt (1938)

How are the voters the rulers of American democracy?

WHAT IS CIVICS POSTTEST

Multiple Choice: Write the letter of the correct answer in each blank. (TEN POINTS EACH)

SS.7.C.2.1 Define the term 'citizen' and identify legal means of becoming a U.S. citizen.

D   1. What is the legal process for becoming a U.S. citizen?
- A. Confederation
- B. Initiation
- C. Mediation
- **D. Naturalization**

B   2. What amendment to the U.S. constitution grants citizenship to any person who is born in the United States, the District of Columbia, or American territories?
- A. 13th Amendment
- **B. 14th Amendment**
- C. 15th Amendment
- D. 16th Amendment

C   3. Which of the following is a qualification for an immigrant to become a U.S. citizen?
- A. Must be 21 years of age or older
- B. Must be able to read and write in two languages
- **C. Must have been a permanent, legal resident for five years**
- D. Must have been a registered voter for at least seven years

C   4. Unlike citizens, resident aliens are not able to _____ in the United States.
- A. Pay taxes
- B. Own property
- **C. Vote in elections**
- D. Attend public schools

A   5. In 1920, which group of Americans gained the right to vote with the Nineteenth Amendment?
- **A. Women**
- B. Hispanics
- C. Residents of Washington, D.C.
- D. Men who did not own property

SS.7.C.2.2 Evaluate the obligations citizens have to obey laws, pay taxes, defend the nation, and serve on juries.

A   6. Which of the following is an example of a U.S. citizen's responsibility?
   A. Vote in elections
   B. Attend school
   C. Obey the law
   D. Pay taxes

A   7. What is the purpose of the Selective Service System (SSS)?
   A. Identifies men who may be eligible to be drafted into military service if needed
   B. Identifies men who may be eligible to serve on a jury for a criminal trial
   C. Identifies men and women who may be needed for public service
   D. Identifies men and women who wish to work in education

B 8. What is the voting age in the United States?
   A. 16
   B. 18
   C. 21
   D. 25

A   9. What is the difference between duties and responsibility?
   A. Duties are actions, like paying taxes, that are required by law.
   B. Duties are actions, like volunteering, that are not required by law.
   C. Duties are actions, like voting, that are required of all U.S. citizens.
   D. Duties are actions, like volunteering, that are not required of all U.S. citizens.

EXTENDED RESPONSE: Use the primary source below to answer the question. (10 POINTS)

"The ultimate rulers of our democracy are not a President and Senators and Congressmen and government officials but the voters of this country." – Franklin D. Roosevelt (1938)

How are the voters the rulers of American democracy?

ANSWERS MAY VARY

FOUNDATIONS OF AMERICAN GOVERNMENT POSTTEST

Multiple Choice: Write the letter of the correct answer in each blank. (FOUR POINTS EACH)

SS.7.C.1.1 Recognize how Enlightenment ideas including Montesquieu's view of separation of powers and John Locke's theories related to natural law and how Locke's social contract influenced the Founding Fathers.

_____ 1. According to Thomas Hobbes' social contract, government protects the rights of the people in exchange for what?
- A. Giving up some freedoms and agreeing to be ruled by government
- B. Giving up all of their freedoms and agreeing to be ruled by government
- C. Giving up some freedoms and agreeing to volunteer for government service
- D. Giving up some freedoms and agreeing to be required to vote in all elections

_____ 2. According to John Locke, where do people get natural rights?
- A. At birth from God
- B. Upon becoming an adult
- C. At birth from government
- D. Upon graduating from high school

_____ 3. What is an example of Baron de Montesquieu's separation of powers?
- A. Limiting the rights of the voters
- B. Creating three branches of government
- C. Having two presidents with equal powers
- D. Dividing national government into regional powers

SS.7.C.1.2 Trace the impact that the Magna Carta, English Bill of Rights, Mayflower Compact, and Thomas Paine's Common Sense had on colonists' views of government.

_____ 4. What New England tradition is related to the concept of self-government that was introduced by the Mayflower Compact?
- A. Town meetings
- B. Political parties
- C. Press conferences
- D. Standing committees

_____ 5. What document was created in 1215 in England to limit the powers of the king?
- A. English Bill of Rights
- B. *Wealth of Nations*
- C. *Common Sense*
- D. Magna Carta

_____ 6. What was Thomas Paine's purpose for writing *Common Sense*?
  A. Inform the American colonists about the importance of trade
  B. Persuade the American colonists to revolt against Britain
  C. Inform the American colonists of revolution in France
  D. Persuade the American colonists to pay taxes

_____ 7. How did the English Bill of Rights influence government?
  A. It ended the death penalty.
  B. It ended the English monarchy.
  C. It gave the elected parliament powers over the king.
  D. It gave the king powers over the elected parliament.

SS.7.C.1.3 Describe how English policies and responses to colonial concerns led to the writing of the Declaration of Independence.

_____ 8. What was one effect of the British winning the French and Indian War?
  A. The British government was interested in fighting the Russians
  B. The British government was forced to leave its American colonies
  C. The British government was richer because the French paid for the war
  D. The British government was in debt because it spent money to pay for the war

_____ 9. How did the American colonists respond to the Stamp Act?
  A. They sent colonists to London to protest outside of the parliament building
  B. They boycotted, or refused to buy, products that were made in Britain
  C. They elected parliament members who were against the Stamp Act
  D. They destroyed the stamps and other government documents

_____ 10. What British law required the American colonists to house British troops?
  A. Townshend Act
  B. Declaratory Act
  C. Quartering Act
  D. Quebec Act

SS.7.C.1.4 Analyze the ideas (natural rights, role of the government) and complaints set forth in the Declaration of Independence.

_____ 11. How was the Declaration of Independence unique, or different, for its time?
  A. It was the first time in history that a nation declared independence
  B. It was the first time that a nation had leaders who studied the Enlightenment
  C. It was the first time that a nation based its power on the consent of its people
  D. It was the first time in history that subjects openly rebelled against their king or queen.

_____ 12. In the Declaration of Independence, 'Life, liberty and the pursuit of happiness' were what type of rights?
  A. Equal
  B. Instituted
  C. Null
  D. Unalienable

_____ 13. The right of the people to abolish, or change, an abusive government is an example of what?
   A. Separation of powers
   B. State of nature
   C. Social contract
   D. Natural law

SS.7.C.3.1 Compare different forms of government (direct democracy, representative democracy, socialism, communism, democracy, autocracy).

_____ 14. The voters of a state voting to ban smoking in public places is an example of what?
   A. Representative democracy
   B. Direct democracy
   C. Authoritarianism
   D. Communism

_____ 15. What do socialism and communism have in common?
   A. Government ownership of resources
   B. Freedom of religion and the press
   C. Regularly scheduled elections
   D. Few limits on businesses

_____ 16. Which of the following describes an authoritarian government?
   A. Rule of law
   B. Free elections
   C. Political parties
   D. State control of media

_____ 17. Which of the following is an example of an autocratic government?
   A. An elected president and Congress
   B. A monarch with an elected parliament
   C. A dictator and appointed military officers
   D. An elected prime minister and parliament

SS.7.C.3.2 Compare parliamentary, federal, confederal, and unitary systems of government.

_____ 18. What is the difference between federal and unitary governments?
   A. In a federal system, the national government can abolish or dissolve its states.
   B. In a unitary system, the national government can abolish or dissolve its states.
   C. In a federal system, the national government has no power over its states.
   D. In a unitary system, the national government has no power over its states.

_____ 19. Which of the following is true of parliamentary governments?
   A. All parliamentary governments have a king or a queen.
   B. There is no direct election of the executive branch by voters.
   C. An Electoral College decides who will serve in the executive branch.
   D. All parliamentary governments have elections every four or five years.

_____ 20. Under what form of government does a group of independent states or countries form an association where the individual states or countries have equal power but the association has little or none?

  A. Confederal
  B. Federal
  C. Parliamentary
  D. Unitary

EXTENDED RESPONSE: Use the primary source below to answer the question. (20 POINTS)

"**That whenever any Form of Government becomes destructive of these ends, it is the Right of the People to alter or to abolish it, and to institute new Government,**" – **Declaration of Independence**

What does this statement have to do with the 'consent of the governed'?

FOUNDATIONS OF AMERICAN GOVERNMENT POSTTEST

Multiple Choice: Write the letter of the correct answer in each blank. (FOUR POINTS EACH)

SS.7.C.1.1 Recognize how Enlightenment ideas including Montesquieu's view of separation of powers and John Locke's theories related to natural law and how Locke's social contract influenced the Founding Fathers.

A   1. According to Thomas Hobbes' social contract, government protects the rights of the people in exchange for what?
   A. Giving up some freedoms and agreeing to be ruled by government
   B. Giving up all of their freedoms and agreeing to be ruled by government
   C. Giving up some freedoms and agreeing to volunteer for government service
   D. Giving up some freedoms and agreeing to be required to vote in all elections

A   2. According to John Locke, where do people get natural rights?
   A. At birth from God
   B. Upon becoming an adult
   C. At birth from government
   D. Upon graduating from high school

B   3. What is an example of Baron de Montesquieu's separation of powers?
   A. Limiting the rights of the voters
   B. Creating three branches of government
   C. Having two presidents with equal powers
   D. Dividing national government into regional powers

SS.7.C.1.2 Trace the impact that the Magna Carta, English Bill of Rights, Mayflower Compact, and Thomas Paine's Common Sense had on colonists' views of government.

A   4. What New England tradition is related to the concept of self-government that was introduced by the Mayflower Compact?
   A. Town meetings
   B. Political parties
   C. Press conferences
   D. Standing committees

D   5. What document was created in 1215 in England to limit the powers of the king?
   A. English Bill of Rights
   B. *Wealth of Nations*
   C. *Common Sense*
   D. Magna Carta

B   6. What was Thomas Paine's purpose for writing *Common Sense*?
- A. Inform the American colonists about the importance of trade
- **B. Persuade the American colonists to revolt against Britain**
- C. Inform the American colonists of revolution in France
- D. Persuade the American colonists to pay taxes

C   7. How did the English Bill of Rights influence government?
- A. It ended the death penalty.
- B. It ended the English monarchy.
- **C. It gave the elected parliament powers over the king.**
- D. It gave the king powers over the elected parliament.

SS.7.C.1.3 Describe how English policies and responses to colonial concerns led to the writing of the Declaration of Independence.

D   8. What was one effect of the British winning the French and Indian War?
- A. The British government was interested in fighting the Russians
- B. The British government was forced to leave its American colonies
- C. The British government was richer because the French paid for the war
- **D. The British government was in debt because it spent money to pay for the war**

B   9. How did the American colonists respond to the Stamp Act?
- A. They sent colonists to London to protest outside of the parliament building
- **B. They boycotted, or refused to buy, products that were made in Britain**
- C. They elected parliament members who were against the Stamp Act
- D. They destroyed the stamps and other government documents

C   10. What British law required the American colonists to house British troops?
- A. Townshend Act
- B. Declaratory Act
- **C. Quartering Act**
- D. Quebec Act

SS.7.C.1.4 Analyze the ideas (natural rights, role of the government) and complaints set forth in the Declaration of Independence.

C   11. How was the Declaration of Independence unique, or different, for its time?
- A. It was the first time in history that a nation declared independence
- B. It was the first time that a nation had leaders who studied the Enlightenment
- **C. It was the first time that a nation based its power on the consent of its people**
- D. It was the first time in history that subjects openly rebelled against their king or queen.

D   12. In the Declaration of Independence, 'Life, liberty and the pursuit of happiness' were what type of rights?
- A. Equal
- B. Instituted
- C. Null
- **D. Unalienable**

C   13. The right of the people to abolish, or change, an abusive government is an example of what?
A. Separation of powers
B. State of nature
C. Social contract
D. Natural law

SS.7.C.3.1 Compare different forms of government (direct democracy, representative democracy, socialism, communism, democracy, autocracy).

B   14. The voters of a state voting to ban smoking in public places is an example of what?
A. Representative democracy
B. Direct democracy
C. Authoritarianism
D. Communism

A   15. What do socialism and communism have in common?
A. Government ownership of resources
B. Freedom of religion and the press
C. Regularly scheduled elections
D. Few limits on businesses

D   16. Which of the following describes an authoritarian government?
A. Rule of law
B. Free elections
C. Political parties
D. State control of media

C   17. Which of the following is an example of an autocratic government?
A. An elected president and Congress
B. A monarch with an elected parliament
C. A dictator and appointed military officers
D. An elected prime minister and parliament

SS.7.C.3.2 Compare parliamentary, federal, confederal, and unitary systems of government.

B   18. What is the difference between federal and unitary governments?
A. In a federal system, the national government can abolish or dissolve its states.
B. In a unitary system, the national government can abolish or dissolve its states.
C. In a federal system, the national government has no power over its states.
D. In a unitary system, the national government has no power over its states.

B   19. Which of the following is true of parliamentary governments?
        A. All parliamentary governments have a king or a queen.
        B. There is no direct election of the executive branch by voters.
        C. An Electoral College decides who will serve in the executive branch.
        D. All parliamentary governments have elections every four or five years.

A   20. Under what form of government does a group of independent states or countries form an association where the individual states or countries have equal power but the association has little or none?
        A. Confederal
        B. Federal
        C. Parliamentary
        D. Unitary

EXTENDED RESPONSE: Use the primary source below to answer the question. (20 POINTS)

"That whenever any Form of Government becomes destructive of these ends, it is the Right of the People to alter or to abolish it, and to institute new Government," – Declaration of Independence

What does this statement have to do with the 'consent of the governed'?

ANSWERS MAY VARY

ROAD TO RATIFICATION POSTTEST

Multiple Choice: Write the letter of the correct answer in each blank. (TEN POINTS EACH)

SS.7.C.1.5 Identify how the weaknesses of the Articles of Confederation led to the writing of the Constitution.

_____ 1. How was Shays' Rebellion an example of the weaknesses of the Articles of Confederation?
- A. The national government had no standing army to maintain law and order.
- B. The national government had too much control over the states.
- C. It was too easy for the national government to raise taxes.
- D. The national government was still as war with Britain.

_____ 2. Why was it difficult to change the Articles of Confederation?
- A. The president of the United States did not want to change the Articles of Confederation.
- B. Any changes to the Articles of Confederation required all thirteen states to agree.
- C. Any changes to the Articles of Confederation required a judge to agree.
- D. The Confederation Congress only met once every three years.

_____ 3. Under the Articles of Confederation, how did the national government raise money?
- A. The national government required states to contribute money every year.
- B. The national government asked states to voluntarily give money.
- C. The national government sold unused land to the Spanish.
- D. The national government taxed imported products.

SS.7.C.1.8 Explain the viewpoints of the Federalists and the Anti-Federalists regarding the ratification of the Constitution and inclusion of a Bill of Rights.

_____ 4. What states supported the New Jersey Plan?
- A. The larger states because it gave them more votes in Congress.
- B. The smaller states because each state had one vote in Congress.
- C. The Southern states because it allowed slaves to count as one person.
- D. The Northern states because it created a Congress that had two houses.

_____ 5. What was one concern that the Anti-Federalists had regarding the Constitution?
- A. The Constitution did not include a Bill of Rights.
- B. The Constitution gave too much power to the states.
- C. The Constitution had no provision for raising money.
- D. The Constitution only had two branches of government.

_____ 6. What was the purpose of the *Federalist Papers*?
   A. To convince the state of Rhode Island to join the Constitutional Convention
   B. To convince the state of North Carolina to support creating a Bill of rights
   C. To convince the state of New Hampshire to repay its wartime debts
   D. To convince the state of New York to ratify the Constitution

_____ 7. What was one result of the Great Compromise?
   A. Each state sent two members to the House of Representatives.
   B. Congress was unicameral, or had one house.
   C. Congress was bicameral, or had two houses.
   D. People elected their Senators.

_____ 8. What did the Constitution create to elect the president and vice president of the United States?
   A. Constitutional Convention
   B. Congressional Committee
   C. Leadership Caucus
   D. Electoral College

EXTENDED REPONSE: Use the primary source below to answer the question. (20 POINTS)

"The injury which may possibly be done by defeating a few good laws, will be amply compensated by the advantage of preventing a number of bad ones." – Alexander Hamilton

What is Alexander Hamilton saying about the power of the veto?

ROAD TO RATIFICATION POSTTEST

Multiple Choice: Write the letter of the correct answer in each blank. (TEN POINTS EACH)

SS.7.C.1.5 Identify how the weaknesses of the Articles of Confederation led to the writing of the Constitution.

A   1. How was Shays' Rebellion an example of the weaknesses of the Articles of Confederation?
   - **A. The national government had no standing army to maintain law and order.**
   - B. The national government had too much control over the states.
   - C. It was too easy for the national government to raise taxes.
   - D. The national government was still as war with Britain.

B   2. Why was it difficult to change the Articles of Confederation?
   - A. The president of the United States did not want to change the Articles of Confederation.
   - **B. Any changes to the Articles of Confederation required all thirteen states to agree.**
   - C. Any changes to the Articles of Confederation required a judge to agree.
   - D. The Confederation Congress only met once every three years.

B   3. Under the Articles of Confederation, how did the national government raise money?
   - A. The national government required states to contribute money every year.
   - **B. The national government asked states to voluntarily give money.**
   - C. The national government sold unused land to the Spanish.
   - D. The national government taxed imported products.

SS.7.C.1.8 Explain the viewpoints of the Federalists and the Anti-Federalists regarding the ratification of the Constitution and inclusion of a Bill of Rights.

B   4. What states supported the New Jersey Plan?
   - A. The larger states because it gave them more votes in Congress.
   - **B. The smaller states because each state had one vote in Congress.**
   - C. The Southern states because it allowed slaves to count as one person.
   - D. The Northern states because it created a Congress that had two houses.

A   5. What was one concern that the Anti-Federalists had regarding the Constitution?
   - **A. The Constitution did not include a Bill of Rights.**
   - B. The Constitution gave too much power to the states.
   - C. The Constitution had no provision for raising money.
   - D. The Constitution only had two branches of government.

D   6. What was the purpose of the *Federalist Papers*?
   - A. To convince the state of Rhode Island to join the Constitutional Convention
   - B. To convince the state of North Carolina to support creating a Bill of rights
   - C. To convince the state of New Hampshire to repay its wartime debts
   - **D. To convince the state of New York to ratify the Constitution**

C   7. What was one result of the Great Compromise?
A. Each state sent two members to the House of Representatives.
B. Congress was unicameral, or had one house.
C. Congress was bicameral, or had two houses.
D. People elected their Senators.

D   8. What did the Constitution create to elect the president and vice president of the United
States?
A. Constitutional Convention
B. Congressional Committee
C. Leadership Caucus
D. Electoral College

EXTENDED REPONSE: Use the primary source below to answer the question. (20 POINTS)

"The injury which may possibly be done by defeating a few good laws, will be amply compensated by the advantage of preventing a number of bad ones." – Alexander Hamilton

What is Alexander Hamilton saying about the power of the veto?

ANSWERS MAY VARY

UNITED STATES CONSTITUTION POSTTEST

Multiple Choice: Write the letter of the correct answer in each blank. (FIVE POINTS EACH)

SS.7.C.3.3 Illustrate the structure and function (three branches of government established in Articles I, II and III with corresponding powers) of government in the United States as established in the Constitution.

_____ 1. Which executive branch office serves as the president of the United States Senate?

    A. Chief Justice

    B. Vice President

    C. Secretary of State

    D. Speaker of the House

_____ 2. What determines the number of representatives each state has in the House of Representatives?

    A. Each state's population determines their representation in the House of Representatives.

    B. Each state's size in square miles determines their representation in the House of Representatives.

    C. Each state's date of statehood determines their representation in the House of Representatives.

    D. Each state's governor determines their representation in the House of Representatives.

_____ 3. The president is responsible for making nominations to the Supreme Court. Who is responsible for confirming, or approving, such nominations?

    A. House of Representatives

    B. Department of Justice

    C. United States Senate

    D. Electoral College

_____ 4. How many years are in the term of office of a United States senator?

    A. Two years

    B. Four years

    C. Six years

    D. Eight years

SS.7.C.3.4 Identify the relationship and division of powers between the federal government and state governments.

_____ 5. What is an example of reserved powers that are set aside only for the states?
   A. Coin money
   B. Declare war
   C. Collect taxes
   D. Conduct elections

_____ 6. What is the 'supremacy clause'?
   A. The supremacy clause states how many members are on the Supreme Court.
   B. The supremacy clause says that the Constitution is the highest law.
   C. The supremacy clause explains who has seniority in government.
   D. The supremacy clause decides who to declare war.

_____ 7. What are concurrent powers?
   A. Powers that are granted by the Constitution to the executive branch.
   B. Powers that are shared by the national and state governments.
   C. Powers that are prohibited by the federal court system.
   D. Powers that are limited to members of Congress.

_____ 8. What is the definition of 'enumerated'?
   A. Listed
   B. Reserved
   C. Shared
   D. Vested

_____ 9. Which of the below is an example of a reserved power?
   A. The federal government setting up an income tax system
   B. The federal government deciding to declare war
   C. The state government establishing new courts
   D. The state government licensing drivers

SS.7.C.3.5 Explain the constitutional amendment process.

Amending the Constitution

Step 1 – Proposing a new amendment	Step 2 – Ratifying a new amendment
?	Three-fourths of the state legislatures ratify the proposed amendment
or	or
Congress calls for a convention after two-thirds of the states petition Congress	Three-fourths of the states ratify the amendment through special constitutional conventions

_____ 10. Choose one of the following to complete the above chart on amending the Constitution:
   A. Three-fourths vote of both houses of Congress
   B. Two-thirds vote of both houses of Congress
   C. Six-tenths vote of both houses of Congress
   D. One-half vote of both houses of Congress

SS.7.C.3.8 Analyze the structure, functions, and processes of the legislative, executive, and judicial branches.

_____ 11. If Congress passes a bill that the president does not like, what can the president do?
   A. The president can order Congress to resign from office.
   B. The president can ask the courts to dismiss the bill.
   C. The president can delete parts of the bill.
   D. The president can veto the bill.

_____ 12. This term is used to describe how the Supreme Court determines if a law is constitutional.
   A. Rule of law
   B. Judicial review
   C. Executive order
   D. Advise and consent

_____ 13. What office in the state of Florida serves as the chief executive?
   A. Governor
   B. Senate president
   C. Speaker of the House
   D. Chief justice of the Supreme Court

_____ 14. If the president vetoes a bill, how can Congress override the president's veto to make the bill into a law?
   A. Either the House of Representatives or the Senate vote to override the veto
   B. Both houses of Congress send a written request to remove the veto
   C. Two-thirds of both houses of Congress vote to override the veto
   D. Congress calls for new elections for the president

_____ 15. What role does a committee have in the lawmaking process?
   A. To determine if a bill is constitutional
   B. To review a bill and send it to the floor for a vote
   C. To work with the president to edit and rewrite the bill
   D. To vote on the bill and send it to the president to sign or veto

EXTENDED RESPONSE: Use the primary source below to answer the question. (25 POINTS)

We the People of the United States, in Order to form a more perfect Union, establish Justice, insure domestic tranquility, provide for the common defence, promote the general Welfare, and secure the Blessings of Liberty to ourselves and our Posterity, do ordain and establish this Constitution for the United States of America.

16. In your opinion, what is the most important purpose of government as detailed in the Preamble of the United States Constitution? Please explain in your own words and use details from the text.

UNITED STATES CONSTITUTION POSTTEST

Multiple Choice: Write the letter of the correct answer in each blank. (FIVE POINTS EACH)

SS.7.C.3.3 Illustrate the structure and function (three branches of government established in Articles I, II and III with corresponding powers) of government in the United States as established in the Constitution.

B   1. Which executive branch office serves as the president of the United States Senate?
   A. Chief Justice
   B. Vice President
   C. Secretary of State
   D. Speaker of the House

A   2. What determines the number of representatives each state has in the House of Representatives?
   A. Each state's population determines their representation in the House of Representatives.
   B. Each state's size in square miles determines their representation in the House of Representatives.
   C. Each state's date of statehood determines their representation in the House of Representatives.
   D. Each state's governor determines their representation in the House of Representatives.

C   3. The president is responsible for making nominations to the Supreme Court. Who is responsible for confirming, or approving, such nominations?
   A. House of Representatives
   B. Department of Justice
   C. United States Senate
   D. Electoral College

C   4. How many years are in the term of office of a United States senator?
   A. Two years
   B. Four years
   C. Six years
   D. Eight years

SS.7.C.3.4 Identify the relationship and division of powers between the federal government and state governments.

D   5. What is an example of reserved powers that are set aside only for the states?
   A. Coin money
   B. Declare war
   C. Collect taxes
   D. Conduct elections

B   6. What is the 'supremacy clause'?
    A. The supremacy clause states how many members are on the Supreme Court.
    B. The supremacy clause says that the Constitution is the highest law.
    C. The supremacy clause explains who has seniority in government.
    D. The supremacy clause decides who to declare war.

B   7. What are concurrent powers?
    A. Powers that are granted by the Constitution to the executive branch.
    B. Powers that are shared by the national and state governments.
    C. Powers that are prohibited by the federal court system.
    D. Powers that are limited to members of Congress.

A   8. What is the definition of 'enumerated'?
    A. Listed
    B. Reserved
    C. Shared
    D. Vested

D   9. Which of the below is an example of a reserved power?
    A. The federal government setting up an income tax system
    B. The federal government deciding to declare war
    C. The state government establishing new courts
    D. The state government licensing drivers

SS.7.C.3.5 Explain the constitutional amendment process.

Amending the Constitution

Step 1 – Proposing a new amendment	Step 2 – Ratifying a new amendment
?	Three-fourths of the state legislatures ratify the proposed amendment
or Congress calls for a convention after two-thirds of the states petition Congress	or Three-fourths of the states ratify the amendment through special constitutional conventions

B   10. Choose one of the following to complete the above chart on amending the Constitution:
    A. Three-fourths vote of both houses of Congress
    B. Two-thirds vote of both houses of Congress
    C. Six-tenths vote of both houses of Congress
    D. One-half vote of both houses of Congress

SS.7.C.3.8 Analyze the structure, functions, and processes of the legislative, executive, and judicial branches.

D 11. If Congress passes a bill that the president does not like, what can the president do?
A. The president can order Congress to resign from office.
B. The president can ask the courts to dismiss the bill.
C. The president can delete parts of the bill.
D. The president can veto the bill.

B 12. This term is used to describe how the Supreme Court determines if a law is constitutional.
A. Rule of law
B. Judicial review
C. Executive order
D. Advise and consent

A 13. What office in the state of Florida serves as the chief executive?
A. Governor
B. Senate president
C. Speaker of the House
D. Chief justice of the Supreme Court

C 14. If the president vetoes a bill, how can Congress override the president's veto to make the bill into a law?
A. Either the House of Representatives or the Senate vote to override the veto
B. Both houses of Congress send a written request to remove the veto
C. Two-thirds of both houses of Congress vote to override the veto
D. Congress calls for new elections for the president

B 15. What role does a committee have in the lawmaking process?
A. To determine if a bill is constitutional
B. To review a bill and send it to the floor for a vote
C. To work with the president to edit and rewrite the bill
D. To vote on the bill and send it to the president to sign or veto

EXTENDED RESPONSE: Use the primary source below to answer the question. (25 POINTS)

> *We the People of the United States, in Order to form a more perfect Union, establish Justice, insure domestic tranquility, provide for the common defence, promote the general Welfare, and secure the Blessings of Liberty to ourselves and our Posterity, do ordain and establish this Constitution for the United States of America.*

16. In your opinion, what is the most important purpose of government as detailed in the Preamble of the United States Constitution? Please explain in your own words and use details from the text.

ANSWERS MAY VARY

NAME   _____

DATE   _____

MOD   _____

AMENDMENTS POSTTEST

Multiple Choice: Write the letter of the correct answer in each blank. (FIVE POINTS EACH)

SS.7.C.2.4 Evaluate rights contained in the Bill of Rights and other amendments to the Constitution.

_____ 1. Which of the following would be a violation of First Amendment rights?

    A. Requiring public school students to recite a Christian prayer at the beginning of every schoo day.

    B. Allowing public school students to organize a prayer group that meets on campus before school.

    C. Offering a high school elective class on religious history that includes the major religions of the world.

    D. Allowing students to sit down during the Pledge of Allegiance if they object to saying the pledge.

_____ 2. If a police officer collects evidence without a warrant, the evidence cannot be used in a court of law. What is this rule called?

    A. Ex post facto

    B. Habeas corpus

    C. Exclusionary Rule

    D. Equal Protection Clause

_____ 3. Which of the following refers to double jeopardy?

    A. Two people being arrested and tried for committing the same crime.

    B. One person being arrested for breaking a law that was not written.

    C. Two people being arrested for the crime of only one person.

    D. One person being tried in court twice for the same crime.

_____ 4. Cutting off someone's hand for stealing would be considered _____ in the United States, and would be in violation of the Eighth Amendment.

    A. Due process

    B. Forced internment

    C. Cruel and unusual punishment

    D. High crimes and misdemeanors

_____ 5. What is required for a police officer to search a person?

    A. Double jeopardy

    B. Excessive force

    C. Probable cause

    D. Voluntary exchange

SS.7.C.2.5 Distinguish how the Constitution safeguards and limits individual rights.

_____ 6. What limit is there to free speech under the First Amendment?
   A. Speech cannot include artistic expression
   B. Speech cannot be offend elected officials
   C. Speech cannot be allowed on public property
   D. Speech cannot create a clear and present danger

_____ 7. Which of the following is a limit to the Second Amendment right to bear arms?
   A. Federal and state governments limiting gun ownership to the military or the police.
   B. Federal and state governments confiscating, or taking away guns without cause.
   C. Federal and state governments requiring a permit to carry a firearm in public.
   D. Federal and state government requiring all citizens to have a firearm.

SS.7.C.3.6 Evaluate Constitutional rights and their impact on individuals and society.

_____ 8. Which of the following is an example of 'probable cause'?
   A. The police checking the shopping bags of every woman leaving a department store.
   B. The police using drug sniffing dogs to search students' gym lockers every day.
   C. The police asking to search a car that matches a description in a robbery.
   D. The police standing guarding a bank for a week after a robbery.

_____ 9. If the state department of transportation offers to buy a home in order to tear it down and expand a highway, this is an example of what?
   A. Grant-in-aid
   B. Eminent domain
   C. Unfunded mandate
   D. Appellate jurisdiction

_____ 10. What does the Ninth Amendment mean when it describes rights that are 'retained' by the people?
   A. The people have the right to hire lawyers when needed.
   B. The people retain the right to defend themselves in a court of law.
   C. The people have rights that are not necessarily listed in the Constitution.
   D. The people retain the right to amend the Constitution every fifteen years.

_____ 11. Sending an email to a school board member asking to change high school hours would be most likely an example of what First Amendment freedom?
   A. Assembly
   B. Petition
   C. Press
   D. Speech

_____ 12. Which of the following is most directly related to the 'assistance of counsel' under the Sixth Amendment?
- A. Public Defender
- B. District Attorney
- C. County Manager
- D. Justice of the Peace

SS.7.C.3.7 Analyze the impact of the 13th, 14th, 15th, 19th, 24th, and 26th amendments on participation of minority groups in the American political process.

_____ 13. After what war were the 13th, 14th and 15th Amendments adopted?
- A. Spanish-American War
- B. Revolutionary War
- C. Korean War
- D. Civil War

_____ 14. Suffragists were notable for their campaign to extend the right to vote to whom?
- A. Young people over the age of 18
- B. Residents of Washington, D.C.
- C. Former slaves
- D. Women

_____ 15. The Fourteenth Amendment's granting of citizenship upon birth was meant to correct what Supreme Court decision?
- A. *Brown v. Board of Education*
- B. *Dred Scott v. Sandford*
- C. *Tinker v. Des Moines*
- D. *Miranda v. Arizona*

EXTENDED REPONSE: Use the primary source below to answer the question. (25 POINTS)

"Who needs the protection of the Bill of Rights most? The weak, the most vulnerable in society."
–Danny Kaye

How does the Bill of Rights protect the rights of the weakest and most vulnerable in society?

AMENDMENTS POSTTEST

Multiple Choice: Write the letter of the correct answer in each blank. (FIVE POINTS EACH)

SS.7.C.2.4 Evaluate rights contained in the Bill of Rights and other amendments to the Constitution.

A   1. Which of the following would be a violation of First Amendment rights?
   A. **Requiring public school students to recite a Christian prayer at the beginning of every school day.**
   B. Allowing public school students to organize a prayer group that meets on campus before school.
   C. Offering a high school elective class on religious history that includes the major religions of the world.
   D. Allowing students to sit down during the Pledge of Allegiance if they object to saying the pledge.

C   2. If a police officer collects evidence without a warrant, the evidence cannot be used in a court of law. What is this rule called?
   A. Ex post facto
   B. Habeas corpus
   C. **Exclusionary Rule**
   D. Equal Protection Clause

D   3. Which of the following refers to double jeopardy?
   A. Two people being arrested and tried for committing the same crime.
   B. One person being arrested for breaking a law that was not written.
   C. Two people being arrested for the crime of only one person.
   D. **One person being tried in court twice for the same crime.**

C   4. Cutting off someone's hand for stealing would be considered _____ in the United States, and would be in violation of the Eighth Amendment.
   A. Due process
   B. Forced internment
   C. **Cruel and unusual punishment**
   D. High crimes and misdemeanors

C   5. What is required for a police officer to search a person?
   A. Double jeopardy
   B. Excessive force
   C. **Probable cause**
   D. Voluntary exchange

SS.7.C.2.5 Distinguish how the Constitution safeguards and limits individual rights.

D   6. What limit is there to free speech under the First Amendment?
       A. Speech cannot include artistic expression
       B. Speech cannot be offend elected officials
       C. Speech cannot be allowed on public property
       D. Speech cannot create a clear and present danger

C   7. Which of the following is a limit to the Second Amendment right to bear arms?
       A. Federal and state governments limiting gun ownership to the military or the police.
       B. Federal and state governments confiscating, or taking away guns without cause.
       C. Federal and state governments requiring a permit to carry a firearm in public.
       D. Federal and state government requiring all citizens to have a firearm.

SS.7.C.3.6 Evaluate Constitutional rights and their impact on individuals and society.

C   8. Which of the following is an example of 'probable cause'?
       A. The police checking the shopping bags of every woman leaving a department store.
       B. The police using drug sniffing dogs to search students' gym lockers every day.
       C. The police asking to search a car that matches a description in a robbery.
       D. The police standing guarding a bank for a week after a robbery.

B   9. If the state department of transportation offers to buy a home in order to tear it down and expand a highway, this is an example of what?
       A. Grant-in-aid
       B. Eminent domain
       C. Unfunded mandate
       D. Appellate jurisdiction

C   10. What does the Ninth Amendment mean when it describes rights that are 'retained' by the people?
       A. The people have the right to hire lawyers when needed.
       B. The people retain the right to defend themselves in a court of law.
       C. The people have rights that are not necessarily listed in the Constitution.
       D. The people retain the right to amend the Constitution every fifteen years.

B   11. Sending an email to a school board member asking to change high school hours would be most likely an example of what First Amendment freedom?
       A. Assembly
       B. Petition
       C. Press
       D. Speech

A   12. Which of the following is most directly related to the 'assistance of counsel' under the Sixth Amendment?
  A. Public Defender
  B. District Attorney
  C. County Manager
  D. Justice of the Peace

SS.7.C.3.7 Analyze the impact of the 13th, 14th, 15th, 19th, 24th, and 26th amendments on participation of minority groups in the American political process.

D   13. After what war were the 13th, 14th and 15th Amendments adopted?
  A. Spanish-American War
  B. Revolutionary War
  C. Korean War
  D. Civil War

D   14. Suffragists were notable for their campaign to extend the right to vote to whom?
  A. Young people over the age of 18
  B. Residents of Washington, D.C.
  C. Former slaves
  D. Women

B   15. The Fourteenth Amendment's granting of citizenship upon birth was meant to correct what Supreme Court decision?
  A. *Brown v. Board of Education*
  B. *Dred Scott v. Sandford*
  C. *Tinker v. Des Moines*
  D. *Miranda v. Arizona*

EXTENDED REPONSE: Use the primary source below to answer the question. (25 POINTS)

> *"Who needs the protection of the Bill of Rights most? The weak, the most vulnerable in society."*
> **–Danny Kaye**

How does the Bill of Rights protect the rights of the weakest and most vulnerable in society?

ANSWERS MAY VARY

NAME _____

DATE _____

MOD _____

LEGISLATIVE AND EXECUTIVE BRANCHES POSTTEST

Multiple Choice: Write the letter of the correct answer in each blank. (FIVE POINTS EACH)

SS.7.C.3.3 Illustrate the structure and function (three branches of government established in Articles ˯ II, and III with corresponding powers) of government in the United States as established by the Constitution.

_____ 1. What executive branch position is appointed by the president?
- A. Speaker of the House of Representatives
- B. President pro tempore of the Senate
- C. Supreme Court justice
- D. Defense secretary

_____ 2. What state has the least members in the House of Representatives?
- A. Alaska
- B. California
- C. Michigan
- D. Texas

_____ 3. What cabinet official is responsible for law enforcement?
- A. Estates general
- B. Solicitor general
- C. Attorney general
- D. Governor general

_____ 4. When House of Representatives and the Senate vote to pass similar bills, in what committee do they work to compromise and create a bill for the president's signature?
- A. Conference committee
- B. Printing committee
- C. Budget committee
- D. Library committee

_____ 5. How many years are in a president's term of office?
- A. Two years
- B. Four years
- C. Six years
- D. Eight years

_____ 6. What member of the cabinet is responsible for executing foreign policy?
   A. Secretary of State
   B. National Security Adviser
   C. Secretary of Homeland Security
   D. Chairman of the Joint Chiefs of Staff

_____ 7. Why would it be more expensive to run for the United States Senate than the House of
Representatives?
   A. The House of Representatives has more members than the Senate.
   B. Senate seats represent an entire state rather than a single House district.
   C. The House of Representatives pays for its candidates' election campaigns.
   D. Senate elections have always been more expensive since the nation's founding.

_____ 8. Congress has not executed this constitutional power since 1959. What power is it?
   A. Raised taxes
   B. Declared war
   C. Appointed judges to the courts
   D. Admitted new states to the Union

_____ 9. How is the Speaker of the House chosen?
   A. The nation's voters elect the Speaker.
   B. Members of the House elect the Speaker.
   C. Members of the majority party select the Speaker of the House.
   D. The President meets with the House members to choose the Speaker.

**SS.7.C.3.8 Analyze the structure, functions, and processes of the legislative, executive, and judicial
branches.**

_____ 10. The president has negotiated a treaty with another country. What is the next step before the
treaty is official?
   A. The president submits the treaty to the Department of Commerce to sign.
   B. The president submits it to the Secretary of State to approve.
   C. The president submits the treaty to the Senate to ratify.
   D. The president submits it to the cabinet to debate.

_____ 11. Why does the United States have a census count of its population every ten years?
   A. To determine how much each state pays in income taxes.
   B. To determine how much taxes pay for education and health.
   C. To determine how many where people live to update mailing lists.
   D. To determine each state's representation in the House of Representatives.

_____ 12. If there is a tie in the Senate, who breaks that tie?
   A. Vice President
   B. Majority Whip
   C. Majority Leader
   D. President Pro Tempore

_____ 13. Which of the following actions require a two-thirds vote in the House of Representatives and the Senate?
- A. Declaring war
- B. Proposing a new budget
- C. Overriding a presidential veto
- D. Confirming presidential appointees

_____ 14. According to the Constitution, how does the United States declare war?
- A. The president and the secretary of defense
- B. Only the president can declare war
- C. Only Congress can declare war
- D. The president and cabinet

_____ 15. Which of these powers are limited to the executive branch?
- A. Taxing imported goods
- B. Pardoning convicted criminals
- C. Establishing new federal courts
- D. Regulating interstate commerce

EXTENDED RESPONSE: Use the primary source below to answer the question. (25 POINTS)

> **"When you get to be President, there are all those things, the honors, the twenty-one gun salutes, all those things. You have to remember it isn't for you. It's for the Presidency."**
>
> **– Harry S. Truman**

What is Harry S. Truman saying about the Presidency in the above quotation?

LEGISLATIVE AND EXECUTIVE BRANCHES POSTTEST

Multiple Choice: Write the letter of the correct answer in each blank. (FIVE POINTS EACH)

SS.7.C.3.3 Illustrate the structure and function (three branches of government established in Articles I, II, and III with corresponding powers) of government in the United States as established by the Constitution.

D   1. What executive branch position is appointed by the president?
  A. Speaker of the House of Representatives
  B. President pro tempore of the Senate
  C. Supreme Court justice
  D. Defense secretary

A   2. What state has the least members in the House of Representatives?
  A. Alaska
  B. California
  C. Michigan
  D. Texas

C   3. What cabinet official is responsible for law enforcement?
  A. Estates general
  B. Solicitor general
  C. Attorney general
  D. Governor general

A   4. When House of Representatives and the Senate vote to pass similar bills, in what committee do they work to compromise and create a bill for the president's signature?
  A. Conference committee
  B. Printing committee
  C. Budget committee
  D. Library committee

B   5. How many years are in a president's term of office?
  A. Two years
  B. Four years
  C. Six years
  D. Eight years

A   6. What member of the cabinet is responsible for executing foreign policy?
  A. Secretary of State
  B. National Security Adviser
  C. Secretary of Homeland Security
  D. Chairman of the Joint Chiefs of Staff

B   7. Why would it be more expensive to run for the United States Senate than the House of Representatives?

     A. The House of Representatives has more members than the Senate.

     B. Senate seats represent an entire state rather than a single House district.

     C. The House of Representatives pays for its candidates' election campaigns.

     D. Senate elections have always been more expensive since the nation's founding.

D   8. Congress has not executed this constitutional power since 1959. What power is it?

     A. Raised taxes

     B. Declared war

     C. Appointed judges to courts

     D. Admitted new states to the Union

B   9. How is the Speaker of the House chosen?

     A. The nation's voters elect the Speaker.

     B. Members of the House elect the Speaker.

     C. Members of the majority party select the Speaker of the House.

     D. The President meets with the House members to choose the Speaker.

SS.7.C.3.8 Analyze the structure, functions, and processes of the legislative, executive, and judicial branches.

C   10. The president has negotiated a treaty with another country. What is the next step before the treaty is official?

     A. The president submits the treaty to the Department of Commerce to sign.

     B. The president submits it to the Secretary of State to approve.

     C. The president submits the treaty to the Senate to ratify.

     D. The president submits it to the cabinet to debate.

D   11. Why does the United States have a census count of its population every ten years?

     A. To determine how much each state pays in income taxes.

     B. To determine how much taxes pay for education and health.

     C. To determine how many where people live to update mailing lists.

     D. To determine each state's representation in the House of Representatives.

A   12. If there is a tie in the Senate, who breaks that tie?

     A. Vice President

     B. Majority Whip

     C. Majority Leader

     D. President Pro Tempore

C   13. Which of the following actions require a two-thirds vote in the House of Representatives and the Senate?

     A. Declaring war

     B. Proposing a new budget

     C. Overriding a presidential veto

     D. Confirming presidential appointees

C   14. According to the Constitution, how does the United States declare war?
   - A. The president and the secretary of defense
   - B. Only the president can declare war
   - **C. Only Congress can declare war**
   - D. The president and cabinet

B   15. Which of these powers are limited to the executive branch?
   - A. Taxing imported goods
   - **B. Pardoning convicted criminals**
   - C. Establishing new federal courts
   - D. Regulating interstate commerce

EXTENDED RESPONSE: Use the primary source below to answer the question (25 POINTS)

> "When you get to be President, there are all those things, the honors, the twenty-one gun salutes, all those things. You have to remember it isn't for you. It's for the Presidency."
>
> – Harry S. Truman

What is Harry S. Truman saying about the Presidency in the above quotation?

ANSWERS MAY VARY

JUDICIAL BRANCH POSTTEST

Multiple Choice: Write the letter of the correct answer in each blank. (EIGHT POINTS EACH)

SS.7.C.3.3 Illustrate the structure and function (three branches of government established in Articles II, and III with corresponding powers) of government in the United States as established by the Constitution.

_____ 1. What government body is responsible for establishing new federal courts?
   A. Court
   B. Congress
   C. Department of State
   D. Department of Justice

_____ 2. What is the difference between Supreme Court justices and the president?
   A. Supreme Court justices cannot be impeached.
   B. Supreme Court justices serve lifetime terms.
   C. Presidents serve up to three terms.
   D. Presidents cannot be impeached.

_____ 3. What does the Constitution say about the federal court system?
   A. It specifically mentions only the Supreme Court.
   B. It mentions the appeals courts and circuit courts.
   C. It mentions the Supreme Court and circuit courts.
   D. It mentions the Supreme Court and appeals courts.

SS.7.C.3.8 Analyze the structure, functions, and processes of the legislative, executive, and judicial branches.

_____ 4. What role did the chief justice of the Supreme Court play in the impeachment trial of President Clinton?
   A. Presented the articles of impeachment to the House Impeachment Committee
   B. Served as the president's defense counsel during the impeachment trial
   C. Served as the presiding judge during the Senate impeachment trial
   D. Presented the case for conviction to the Senate impeachment trial

_____ 5. A court ruling from the past that influences modern court rulings is known as what?
   A. Consent
   B. Litigant
   C. Patent
   D. Precedent

SS.7.C.3.12 Analyze the significance and outcomes of landmark Supreme Court cases including, but not limited to, *Marbury v. Madison, Plessy v. Ferguson, Brown v. Board of Education, Gideon v. Wainright, Miranda v. Arizona, In re: Gault, Tinker v. Des Moines, Hazelwood v. Kuhlmeier, United States v. Nixon, and Bush v. Gore*.

_____ 6. How is judicial review created by *Marbury v. Madison*?
    A. It allows the president to approve or reject Supreme Court rulings.
    B. It allows the Senate to review presidential nominees to the court system.
    C. It allows the attorney general to interview presidential nominees to the court system.
    D. It allows the Supreme Court to have the final word on whether laws are constitutional.

_____ 7. "You have the right to remain silent," is part of what are called the 'Miranda Rights' read to the accused under Miranda v. Arizona. What rights are being protected by the Miranda Rights?
    A. The right against unreasonable searches
    B. The right not to be assigned excessive bail
    C. The right to be tried by a jury of one's peers
    D. The right not to be forced to testify against oneself

SS.7.C.3.10 Identify sources and types (civil, criminal, constitutional, military) of law.

_____ 8. A civil case brought before a civil court is what?
    A. Felony
    B. Lawsuit
    C. Misdemeanor
    D. Subpoena

_____ 9. Who serves as the plaintiff in a criminal trial?
    A. The Victim
    B. The Lawyer
    C. The Defendant
    D. The Government

_____ 10. What type of court is unique to military law?
    A. Special prosecutor
    B. Superior Court
    C. Court martial
    D. Grand Jury

EXTENDED RESPONSE (20 POINTS)

Should Supreme Court justices be permitted to serve lifetime terms? Please explain why or why not.

JUDICIAL BRANCH POSTTEST

Multiple Choice: Write the letter of the correct answer in each blank. (EIGHT POINTS EACH)

SS.7.C.3.3 Illustrate the structure and function (three branches of government established in Articles II, and III with corresponding powers) of government in the United States as established by the Constitution.

B   1. What government body is responsible for establishing new federal courts?
- A. Court
- **B. Congress**
- C. Department of State
- D. Department of Justice

B   2. What is the difference between Supreme Court justices and the president?
- A. Supreme Court justices cannot be impeached.
- **B. Supreme Court justices serve lifetime terms.**
- C. Presidents serve up to three terms.
- D. Presidents cannot be impeached.

A   3. What does the Constitution say about the federal court system?
- **A. It specifically mentions only the Supreme Court.**
- B. It mentions the appeals courts and circuit courts.
- C. It mentions the Supreme Court and circuit courts.
- D. It mentions the Supreme Court and appeals courts.

SS.7.C.3.8 Analyze the structure, functions, and processes of the legislative, executive, and judicial branches.

C   4. What role did the chief justice of the Supreme Court play in the impeachment trial of President Clinton?
- A. Presented the articles of impeachment to the House Impeachment Committee
- B. Served as the president's defense counsel during the impeachment trial
- **C. Served as the presiding judge during the Senate impeachment trial**
- D. Presented the case for conviction to the Senate impeachment trial

D   5. A court ruling from the past that influences modern court rulings is known as what?
- A. Consent
- B. Litigant
- C. Patent
- **D. Precedent**

SS.7.C.3.12 Analyze the significance and outcomes of landmark Supreme Court cases including, but not limited to, *Marbury v. Madison, Plessy v. Ferguson, Brown v. Board of Education, Gideon v. Wainright, Miranda v. Arizona, In re: Gault, Tinker v. Des Moines, Hazelwood v. Kuhlmeier, United States v. Nixon,* and *Bush v. Gore*.

D   6. How is judicial review created by *Marbury v. Madison*?
    A. It allows the president to approve or reject Supreme Court rulings.
    B. It allows the Senate to review presidential nominees to the court system.
    C. It allows the attorney general to interview presidential nominees to the court system.
    D. It allows the Supreme Court to have the final word on whether laws are constitutional.

D   7. "You have the right to remain silent," is part of what are called the 'Miranda Rights' read to the accused under Miranda v. Arizona. What rights are being protected by the Miranda Rights?
    A. The right against unreasonable searches
    B. The right not to be assigned excessive bail
    C. The right to be tried by a jury of one's peers
    D. The right not to be forced to testify against oneself

SS.7.C.3.10 Identify sources and types (civil, criminal, constitutional, military) of law

B   8. A civil case brought before a civil court is what?
    A. Felony
    B. Lawsuit
    C. Misdemeanor
    D. Subpoena

D   9. Who serves as the plaintiff in a criminal trial?
    A. The Victim
    B. The Lawyer
    C. The Defendant
    D. The Government

C   10. What type of court is unique to military law?
    A. Special prosecutor
    B. Superior Court
    C. Court martial
    D. Grand Jury

EXTENDED RESPONSE (20 POINTS)

Should Supreme Court justices be permitted to serve lifetime terms? Please explain why or why not.

ANSWERS MAY VARY

NAME _____

DATE _____

MOD _____

STATE AND LOCAL GOVERNMENTS POSTTEST

Multiple Choice: Write the letter of the correct answer in each blank. (TEN POINTS EACH)

SS.7.C.3.4 Identify the relationship and division of powers between federal government and state governments.

_____ 1. What is an example of an unfunded mandate?
   A. The states ask to pay higher taxes into the federal treasury
   B. The federal government building a new highway without tolls.
   C. The states ask the federal government to create a new program.
   D. The federal government creating a new program the states pay for.

_____ 2. What does 'reserved powers' refer to in the Tenth Amendment?
   A. Powers that are reserved for the federal, or national, government
   B. Powers that are reserved for the state governments and people
   C. Powers that are restricted to elected officials
   D. Powers that are restricted to the voters

_____ 3. Which of the following activities are connected with expressed powers?
   A. Regulate foreign commerce
   B. Protect public safety
   C. Administer elections
   D. Borrow money

SS.7.C.3.9 Illustrate the lawmaking process at the local, state, and federal levels.

_____ 4. What power do state governors have in common with the president?
   A. The power to amend the Constitution
   B. The power to send troops overseas
   C. The power to veto legislation
   D. The power to declare war

SS.7.C.3.11 Diagram the levels, functions, and powers of courts at the state and federal levels.

_____ 5. How are local trial court judges chosen?
   A. A local commission nominates them
   B. The sheriff appoints them
   C. The mayor appoints them
   D. The voters elect them

SS.7.C.3.13 Compare the constitutions of the United States and Florida.

_____ 6. The _____ is to the State of Florida what the vice president is to the United States.
   A. Vice governor
   B. House speaker
   C. Sergeant-at-arms
   D. Lieutenant governor

_____ 7. How are the constitutions of the United States and Florida different?
   A. The chief executive is limited to two terms in office.
   B. The chief executive appoints Supreme Court justices.
   C. Members of the state cabinet are elected by the people.
   D. Members of the federal cabinet are elected by the people.

_____ 8. What are the political subdivisions, or units, of Florida called?
   A. Boroughs
   B. Counties
   C. Parishes
   D. Provinces

SS.7.C.3.14 Differentiate between local, state, and federal governments' obligations and services.

_____ 9. Which of the following are examples of local government responsibilities?
   A. Collecting garbage, building schools, and operating libraries
   B. Running post offices, printing money, and building schools
   C. Printing money, raising troops, and collecting garbage.
   D. Raising troops, printing money, and building schools

_____ 10. What state official serves as the chief law enforcement officer?
   A. State attorney
   B. District attorney
   C. Attorney general
   D. Inspector general

STATE AND LOCAL GOVERNMENTS POSTTEST

Multiple Choice: Write the letter of the correct answer in each blank. (TEN POINTS EACH)

SS.7.C.3.4 Identify the relationship and division of powers between federal government and state governments.

D   1. What is an example of an unfunded mandate?
- A. The states ask to pay higher taxes into the federal treasury
- B. The federal government building a new highway without tolls.
- C. The states ask the federal government to create a new program.
- **D. The federal government creating a new program the states must pay for.**

B   2. What does 'reserved powers' refer to in the Tenth Amendment?
- A. Powers that are reserved for the federal, or national, government
- **B. Powers that are reserved for the state governments and people**
- C. Powers that are restricted to elected officials
- D. Powers that are restricted to the voters

A   3. Which of the following activities are connected with expressed powers?
- **A. Regulate foreign commerce**
- B. Protect public safety
- C. Administer elections
- D. Borrow money

SS.7.C.3.9 Illustrate the lawmaking process at the local, state, and federal levels.

C   4. What power do state governors have in common with the president?
- A. The power to amend the Constitution
- B. The power to send troops overseas
- **C. The power to veto legislation**
- D. The power to declare war

SS.7.C.3.11 Diagram the levels, functions, and powers of courts at the state and federal levels.

D   5. How are local trial court judges chosen?
- A. A local commission nominates them
- B. The sheriff appoints them
- C. The mayor appoints them
- **D. The voters elect them**

SS.7.C.3.13 Compare the constitutions of the United States and Florida.

D   6. The _____ is to the State of Florida what the vice president is to the United States.
- A. Vice governor
- B. House speaker
- C. Sergeant-at-arms
- **D. Lieutenant governor**

C   7. How are the constitutions of the United States and Florida different?
- A. The chief executive is limited to two terms in office.
- B. The chief executive appoints Supreme Court justices.
- **C. Members of the state cabinet are elected by the people.**
- D. Members of the federal cabinet are elected by the people.

B   8. What are the political subdivisions, or units, of Florida called?
- A. Boroughs
- **B. Counties**
- C. Parishes
- D. Provinces

SS.7.C.3.14 Differentiate between local, state, and federal governments' obligations and services.

A   9. Which of the following are examples of local government responsibilities?
- **A. Collecting garbage, building schools, and operating libraries**
- B. Running post offices, printing money, and building schools
- C. Printing money, raising troops, and collecting garbage.
- D. Raising troops, printing money, and building schools

C   10. What state official serves as the chief law enforcement officer?
- A. State attorney
- B. District attorney
- **C. Attorney general**
- D. Inspector general

POLITICAL PROCESS POSTTEST

Multiple Choice: Write the letter of the correct answer in each blank. (TEN POINTS EACH)

SS.7.C.2.10 Examine the impact of media, individuals, and interest groups on monitoring and influencing government.

_____ 1. Which of the following is an example of the watchdog role played by the media?
- A. A news story about local transportation.
- B. A news story about government corruption.
- C. A news story about the latest movie release.
- D. A news story about the opening of a new school.

_____ 2. What is the goal of interest groups?
- A. To join people with similar interests to unite to promote their beliefs.
- B. To raise money for expensive elections and to defeat opponents
- C. To find tax-free ways to speak out on political issues.
- D. To find people to run for public office.

SS.7.C.2.11 Analyze media and political communications (bias, symbolism, propaganda).

_____ 3. "Everybody is going to the game" is an example of what propaganda?
- A. Glittering generalities
- B. Celebrity testimonial
- C. Bandwagon claims
- D. Straw man

SS.7.C.2.13 Examine multiple perspectives on public and current issues.

Below are views for and against lowering the drinking age to 18.

1. If a young adult can vote in elections and serve in the military, it makes sense that the drinking age should be 18.	2. It is harmful for teenagers to consume alcohol at a time when their brains are still developing. They should wait until they are truly adults at 21 years of age.

_____ 4. What conclusion can be drawn from these two statements?
- A. The drinking age is too low.
- B. Military service is important.
- C. People disagree about who is an adult.
- D. There are problems with teenagers voting.

SS.7.C.2.8 Identify America's current political parties, and illustrate their ideas about government.

_____ 5. Which statement reflects Republicans views on government?
  A. Higher taxes leads to a better-run government.
  B. Lower taxes lead to a better-run government.
  C. Cutting military spending is good policy.
  D. Increased regulation is good policy.

_____ 6. What role do the national political party conventions play in national politics?
  A. They propose new constitutional amendments.
  B. They help nominate candidates for president.
  C. They help nominate candidates for governor.
  D. They propose new federal statutes.

SS.7.C.2.9 Evaluate candidates for political office by analyzing their qualifications, experience, issue-based platforms, debates, and political ads.

Below is information about a candidate for public office.

John Davis for County Sheriff

John Davis has been a county deputy for over 30 years.
John Davis wants to keep our community safe.
John Davis needs your support on Election Day!

_____ 7. What does this campaign advertisement say about John Davis?
  A. He is running on his experience as a county deputy.
  B. He believes that his opponent will not be a good sheriff.
  C. He believes that crime is the number one problem in the county.
  D. He is running because he is the only candidate who is a county deputy.

Below is information about two candidates for public office.

Joe Smith for Congress	Ann Green for Congress
Joe wants to bring our troops home. Joe wants to save the environment. Joe wants to build more schools.	Ann wants to cut taxes. Ann wants to create more jobs for working Americans. Ann wants to build a strong military.

_____ 8. Based on the above information, which interest group is more likely to support Joe Smith for Congress?
- A. National Organization for Women
- B. American Medical Association
- C. U.S. Chamber of Commerce
- D. World Wildlife Federation

EXTENDED RESPONSE (20 POINTS)

Besides the constitutionally required qualifications, what three qualities should someone have in order to be president? Please explain your choices.

ANSWERS MAY VARY

POLITICAL PROCESS POSTTEST

Multiple Choice: Write the letter of the correct answer in each blank. (TEN POINTS EACH)

SS.7.C.2.10 Examine the impact of media, individuals, and interest groups on monitoring and influencing government.

B   1. Which of the following is an example of the watchdog role played by the media?
- A. A news story about local transportation.
- **B. A news story about government corruption.**
- C. A news story about the latest movie release.
- D. A news story about the opening of a new school.

A   2. What is the goal of interest groups?
- **A. To join people with similar interests to unite to promote their beliefs.**
- B. To raise money for expensive elections and to defeat opponents
- C. To find tax-free ways to speak out on political issues.
- D. To find people to run for public office.

SS.7.C.2.11 Analyze media and political communications (bias, symbolism, propaganda).

C   3. "Everybody is going to the game" is an example of what propaganda?
- A. Glittering generalities
- B. Celebrity testimonial
- **C. Bandwagon claims**
- D. Straw man

SS.7.C.2.13 Examine multiple perspectives on public and current issues.

Below are views for and against lowering the drinking age to 18.

3. If a young adult can vote in elections and serve in the military, it makes sense that the drinking age should be 18.	4. It is harmful for teenagers to consume alcohol at a time when their brains are still developing. They should wait until they are truly adults at 21 years of age.

C   4. What conclusion can be drawn from these two statements?
- A. The drinking age is too low.
- B. Military service is important.
- **C. People disagree about who is an adult.**
- D. There are problems with teenagers voting.

SS.7.C.2.8 Identify America's current political parties, and illustrate their ideas about government.

B   5. Which statement reflects Republicans views on government?
         A.   Higher taxes leads to a better-run government.
         B.   Lower taxes lead to a better-run government.
         C.   Cutting military spending is good policy.
         D.   Increased regulation is good policy.

B   6. What role do the national political party conventions play in national politics?
         A.   They propose new constitutional amendments.
         B.   They help nominate candidates for president.
         C.   They help nominate candidates for governor.
         D.   They propose new federal statutes.

SS.7.C.2.9 Evaluate candidates for political office by analyzing their qualifications, experience, issue-based platforms, debates, and political ads.

Below is information about a candidate for public office.

John Davis for County Sheriff

John Davis has been a county deputy for over 30 years.
John Davis wants to keep our community safe.
John Davis needs your support on Election Day!

A   7. What does this campaign advertisement say about John Davis?
         A.   He is running on his experience as a county deputy.
         B.   He believes that his opponent will not be a good sheriff.
         C.   He believes that crime is the number one problem in the county.
         D.   He is running because he is the only candidate who is a county deputy.

Below is information about two candidates for public office.

Joe Smith for Congress	Ann Green for Congress
Joe wants to bring our troops home. Joe wants to save the environment. Joe wants to build more schools.	Ann wants to cut taxes. Ann wants to create more jobs for working Americans. Ann wants to build a strong military.

D   8. Based on the above information, which interest group is more likely to support Joe Smith for Congress?
   A.   National Organization for Women
   B.   American Medical Association
   C.   U.S. Chamber of Commerce
   D.   World Wildlife Federation

EXTENDED RESPONSE (20 POINTS)

Besides the constitutionally required qualifications, what three qualities should someone have in order to be president? Please explain your choices.

ANSWERS MAY VARY

NAME   _____

DATE   _____

MOD   _____

FOREIGN POLICY POSTTEST

Multiple Choice: Write the letter of the correct answer in each blank. (TEN POINTS EACH)

SS.7.C.4.1 Differentiate concepts related to U.S. domestic and foreign policy.

_____ 1. Which of the following actions is an example of Congressional involvement in foreign policy?

     A. The Senate ratifying international treaties.

     B. The Senate appointing a secretary of state.

     C. The House of Representatives ratifying international treaties.

     D. The House of Representatives appointing a secretary of state.

_____ 2. Which of the following is an example of a president's foreign policy?

     A. Opening a new military base in Maine

     B. Meeting with the governor of New Mexico

     C. Helping to negotiate peace in Northern Ireland

     D. Working with Congress to change naturalization rules

_____ 3. According to the Constitution, which of the following can the president do?

     A. Declare war

     B. Appoint ambassadors

     C. Grant titles of nobility

     D. Hear legal cases involving foreign nations

SS.7.C.4.2 Recognize government and citizen participation in international organizations.

_____ 4. The Red Cross and UNICEF are examples of what types of organizations?

     A. Trade organizations

     B. Foreign organizations

     C. Mutual defense organizations

     D. Non-governmental organizations

_____ 5. What international organization, organized after World War II, meets regularly in New York City?

     A. United Nations

     B. League of Nations

     C. World Trade Organization

     D. North Atlantic Treaty Organization

SS.7.C.4.3 Describe examples of how the United States has dealt with international conflicts.

_____ 6. What is the purpose of economic sanctions against a hostile nation?
    A. To build up a stronger military
    B. To spark an international economic downturn
    C. To weaken an enemy nation's economy and avoid war
    D. To strengthen an enemy nation's economy and cause war

_____ 7. In his Farewell Address, George Washington warned against 'foreign entanglements.' What belief system would agree with Washington?
    A. Individualism
    B. Internationalism
    C. Interventionism
    D. Isolationism

_____ 8. When the United States closed its embassy in Cuba, what did this mean?
    A. The United States was cutting off normal relations with Cuba.
    B. The United States could not afford to keep an embassy.
    C. The United States was declaring war on Cuba.
    D. The United States supported communism.

EXTENDED RESPONSE (20 POINTS)

Should the United States become more or less involved in international issues? Explain your answer.

FOREIGN POLICY POSTTEST

Multiple Choice: Write the letter of the correct answer in each blank. (TEN POINTS EACH)

SS.7.C.4.1 Differentiate concepts related to U.S. domestic and foreign policy.

A   1. Which of the following actions is an example of Congressional involvement in foreign policy?
  - **A. The Senate ratifying international treaties.**
  - B. The Senate appointing a secretary of state.
  - C. The House of Representatives ratifying international treaties.
  - D. The House of Representatives appointing a secretary of state.

C   2. Which of the following is an example of a president's foreign policy?
  - A. Opening a new military base in Maine
  - B. Meeting with the governor of New Mexico
  - **C. Helping to negotiate peace in Northern Ireland**
  - D. Working with Congress to change naturalization rules

B   3. According to the Constitution, which of the following can the president do?
  - A. Declare war
  - **B. Appoint ambassadors**
  - C. Grant titles of nobility
  - D. Hear legal cases involving foreign nations

SS.7.C.4.2 Recognize government and citizen participation in international organizations.

D   4. The Red Cross and UNICEF are examples of what types of organizations?
  - A. Trade organizations
  - B. Foreign organizations
  - C. Mutual defense organizations
  - **D. Non-governmental organizations**

A
City?   5. What international organization, organized after World War II, meets regularly in New York City?
  - **A. United Nations**
  - B. League of Nations
  - C. World Trade Organization
  - D. North Atlantic Treaty Organization

SS.7.C.4.3 Describe examples of how the United States has dealt with international conflicts.

C   6. What is the purpose of economic sanctions against a hostile nation?
- A. To build up a stronger military
- B. To spark an international economic downturn
- **C. To weaken an enemy nation's economy and avoid war**
- D. To strengthen an enemy nation's economy and cause war

D   7. In his Farewell Address, George Washington warned against 'foreign entanglements.' What belief system would agree with Washington?
- A. Individualism
- B. Internationalism
- C. Interventionism
- **D. Isolationism**

A   8. When the United States closed its embassy in Cuba, what did this mean?
- **A. The United States was cutting off normal relations with Cuba.**
- B. The United States could not afford to keep an embassy.
- C. The United States was declaring war on Cuba.
- D. The United States supported communism.

EXTENDED RESPONSE (20 POINTS)

Should the United States become more or less involved in international issues? Explain your answer.

ANSWERS MAY VARY

NAME _____
DATE _____
MOD _____

FREE MIXED MARKET ECONOMY POSTTEST

Multiple Choice: Write the letter of the correct answer in each blank (TEN POINTS EACH)

SS.7.E.1.1 Explain how the principles of a market and mixed economy helped to develop the United States into a democratic nation.

_____ 1. Which of the following is an example of a mixed market economy?
    A. Government planners control all industry.
    B. Individuals and businesses own the resources.
    C. Families and background determine individuals' careers.
    D. Government plays a role in but does not dominate industry.

_____ 2. A trade union would represent which sector of the mixed market economy?
    A. Capital
    B. Consumers
    C. Government
    D. Labor

_____ 3. How do the principles of a mixed economy relate to a democratic system of government?
    A. The government raises taxes and fees as necessary.
    B. The government guarantees success of failure of business.
    C. Consumers vote with their dollars for products and services.
    D. Consumers vote for elected officials who support capitalism.

SS.7.E.1.3 Review the concepts of supply and demand, choice, scarcity, and opportunity cost as they relate to the development of the mixed market economy in the United States.

_____ 4. Which of the following events would cause supply to drop?
    A. The hiring of new workers at a toy factory.
    B. An increase in the price of steel for manufacturing.
    C. The discovery of a new oil deposit in the Gulf of Mexico.
    D. A drought that kills a significant percentage of the cotton crop.

_____ 5. When presented with the choice of either building a new highway or opening a new university, a state decides to build a new highway. The decision not to open a new university is an example of what?
    A. Benefit-cost analysis
    B. Marginal revenue
    C. Opportunity cost
    D. Variable cost

_____ 6. A government creating a budget to determine how to spend its money is an example of what concept?
   A. Scarcity
   B. Shortage
   C. Supply
   D. Surplus

SS.7.E.1.5 Assess how profits, incentives, and competition motivate individuals, households, and businesses in a free market economy.

_____ 7. Which of the following would damage or harm the profit motive?
   A. Voluntary exchange
   B. Free enterprise
   C. Price controls
   D. Free markets

_____ 8. What happens in the absence of competition?
   A. Capitalism
   B. Incentive
   C. Monopoly
   D. Specialization

SS.7.E.2.1 Explain how federal, state, and local taxes support the economy as a function of the U.S. government.

_____ 9. What level of government relies mainly on property taxes to fund its budget?
   A. Federal
   B. Interstate
   C. Local
   D. State

_____ 10. How does the federal government differ from most state governments?
   A. The state governments are not required to balance their budgets.
   B. The federal government is not required to balance its budget.
   C. Only the state governments have an income tax for revenue.
   D. The federal government has a sales tax to raise revenue.

FREE MIXED MARKET ECONOMY POSTTEST

Multiple Choice: Write the letter of the correct answer in each blank (TEN POINTS EACH)

SS.7.E.1.1 Explain how the principles of a market and mixed economy helped to develop the United States into a democratic nation.

D   1. Which of the following is an example of a mixed market economy?
   A. Government planners control all industry.
   B. Individuals and businesses own the resources.
   C. Families and background determine individuals' careers.
   D. Government plays a role in but does not dominate industry.

D   2. A trade union would represent which sector of the mixed market economy?
   A. Capital
   B. Consumers
   C. Government
   D. Labor

C   3. How do the principles of a mixed economy relate to a democratic system of government?
   A. The government raises taxes and fees as necessary.
   B. The government guarantees success of failure of business.
   C. Consumers vote with their dollars for products and services.
   D. Consumers vote for elected officials who support capitalism.

SS.7.E.1.3 Review the concepts of supply and demand, choice, scarcity, and opportunity cost as they relate to the development of the mixed market economy in the United States.

D   4. Which of the following events would cause supply to drop?
   A. The hiring of new workers at a toy factory.
   B. An increase in the price of steel for manufacturing.
   C. The discovery of a new oil deposit in the Gulf of Mexico.
   D. A drought that kills a significant percentage of the cotton crop.

C   5. When presented with the choice of either building a new highway or opening a new university, a state decides to build a new highway. The decision not to open a new university is an example of what?
   A. Benefit-cost analysis
   B. Marginal revenue
   C. Opportunity cost
   D. Variable cost

A   6. A government creating a budget to determine how to spend its money is an example of what concept?
   A. Scarcity
   B. Shortage
   C. Supply
   D. Surplus

SS.7.E.1.5 Assess how profits, incentives, and competition motivate individuals, households, and businesses in a free market economy.

C   7. Which of the following would damage or harm the profit motive?
   A. Voluntary exchange
   B. Free enterprise
   C. Price controls
   D. Free markets

C   8. What happens in the absence of competition?
   A. Capitalism
   B. Incentive
   C. Monopoly
   D. Specialization

SS.7.E.2.1 Explain how federal, state, and local taxes support the economy as a function of the U.S. government.

C   9. What level of government relies mainly on property taxes to fund its budget?
   A. Federal
   B. Interstate
   C. Local
   D. State

B   10. How does the federal government differ from most state governments?
   A. The state governments are not required to balance their budgets.
   B. The federal government is not required to balance its budget.
   C. Only the state governments have an income tax for revenue.
   D. The federal government has a sales tax to raise revenue.

FINANCIAL INSTITUTIONS POSTTEST

Multiple Choice: Write the letter of the correct answer in each blank. (20 POINTS EACH)

SS.7.E.1.2 Discuss the importance of borrowing and lending in the United States, the government's role in controlling financial institutions, and list the advantages and disadvantages of using credit.

_____ 1. How does a budget surplus help reduce debt?
   A. Budget surplus means that the debt is eliminated.
   B. Budget surplus means that the budget is balanced.
   C. Budget surplus allows for higher taxes to pay down the debt.
   D. Budget surplus allows for the extra money to pay down the debt.

SS.7.E.1.4 Discuss the function of financial institutions in the development of a market economy.

_____ 2. What is the difference between checking and savings accounts?
   A. Money from checking accounts does not earn interest.
   B. Money from savings accounts does not earn interest.
   C. Money from checking accounts earns more interest.
   D. Money from savings accounts earns more interest.

_____ 3. What did the government due in response to the Great Depression lowering public confidence in banks?
   A. Established the Federal Deposit Insurance Corporation
   B. Established the Department of the Treasury
   C. Established the Federal Reserve Bank
   D. Established credit unions

SS.7.E.1.6 Compare the national budget process to the personal budget process.

_____ 4. According to the Constitution, all spending bills originate where?
   A. Senate
   B. President
   C. Secretary of the Treasury
   D. House of Representatives

SS.7.E.2.2 Describe the banking system in the United States and its impact on the money supply.

_____ 5. How does the Federal Reserve System function?
   A. As a national bank
   B. As an emergency lender
   C. As an insurance company
   D. As an investment corporation

FINANCIAL INSTITUTIONS POSTTEST

Multiple Choice: Write the letter of the correct answer in each blank. (20 POINTS EACH)

SS.7.E.1.2 Discuss the importance of borrowing and lending in the United States, the government's role in controlling financial institutions, and list the advantages and disadvantages of using credit.

C   1. How does a budget surplus help reduce debt?
   A. Budget surplus means that the debt is eliminated.
   B. Budget surplus means that the budget is balanced.
   C. Budget surplus allows for higher taxes to pay down the debt.
   D. Budget surplus allows for the extra money to pay down the debt.

SS.7.E.1.4 Discuss the function of financial institutions in the development of a market economy.

D   2. What is the difference between checking and savings accounts?
   A. Money from checking accounts does not earn interest.
   B. Money from savings accounts does not earn interest.
   C. Money from checking accounts earns more interest.
   D. Money from savings accounts earns more interest.

A   3. What did the government due in response to the Great Depression lowering public confidence in banks?
   A. Established the Federal Deposit Insurance Corporation
   B. Established the Department of the Treasury
   C. Established the Federal Reserve Bank
   D. Established credit unions

SS.7.E.1.6 Compare the national budget process to the personal budget process.

D   4. According to the Constitution, all spending bills originate where?
   A. Senate
   B. President
   C. Secretary of the Treasury
   D. House of Representatives

SS.7.E.2.2 Describe the banking system in the United States and its impact on the money supply.

A   5. How does the Federal Reserve System function?
   A. As a national bank
   B. As an emergency lender
   C. As an insurance company
   D. As an investment corporation

Made in United States
Orlando, FL
18 January 2025

57407221R00037